AF485923

Cary Trudell

Historically:
One ounce of silver is equivalent to 10 days of stored labor.

* * * * * * *

Please look for my other Titles:

1. Natural Forces: Inspired Poems
About The Natural World

2. Total Control: Tales Of Travel
Through Time And Space

3. Rhood's Return (a short story taken
from Total Control, 1st of a trilogy)

4. Manifesting Abundance: How To Think
Abundance Into Your Life

and
5. Heaven, Hell, On Earth We Dwell:
Faith On Fire Biblically Inspired Poetry

* * * * * * *

PYRAMID OF POWER SET RANKINGS:

VALUING YOUR SILVER SHIELD GROUP POP COINS

THIS BOOK IS DEDICATED TO POP STACKERS EVERYWHERE

I STACK
THEREFORE I AM

PYRAMID OF POWER SET RANKINGS:

VALUING YOUR SILVER SHIELD GROUP POP COINS

BY CARY TRUDELL

© 2017, 2022

INDEPENDENTLY PUBLISHED
ISBN: 9798837860577
ASIN: B082NZVLP3

TABLE OF CONTENTS:

Page Number   **Section Title**

SILVER IS CURRENTLY THE GREATEST INVESTMENT OPPORTUNITY IN THE HISTORY OF HUMANITY

INTRODUCTION ~ HOW THIS GUIDE CAME ABOUT:

Hello fellow silver stacker, I pray your day is blessed. I trust you have come across this short informative guide to determining the relative value of Silver Shield Group (SSG) Pyramid Of Power (POP) coin Sets because you either own some or all of the coins or else you may have heard about them and may have an interest in purchasing some of them either now or sometime in the future. Whatever the reason for your interest in this guide I welcome you to its contents and hope and trust you will find great value here.

In my estimation, this guide is both long overdue and awaited by many avid collectors, even it they didn't know they would find interest in it. It could likened to the idea that, "You didn't know it was missing from your life until you discovered it." At least it will be for some; for others it will be entertainment or something useful and interesting to contemplate, and perhaps, replicate.

Let me be clear from the start: **This Guide regards ONLY the ORIGINAL series of SSG Pyramid Of Power coins and does NOT cover VERSION 2 at all.** However, it can be used as a template to create a separate, unique guide for Version 2, just as it can for any SSG series.

I used to be a member of Chris Duane's Silver Shield Group for several years. Though I've never met him in person, I consider Chris to be a good friend whom I have called many times a 'Silver Visionary.' His ideas for coin designs and the subsequent coins he has minted are brilliant and amazing, absolutely the finest coins on the market. I'm currently not a member of the group but I may rejoin one day. While I was there I collected all of the coins from the original Pyramid Of Power coin series that he minted, both Proofs and BU, and built a complete SET.

I was an avid silver collector with no intention of selling any of my silver. But times changed and I began selling some of my 'stack' on eBay as well as to silver dealers such as Provident Metals, SDBullion and JMBullion.

In my estimation, selling coin series as a SET is very intelligent and a great way to cut unnecessary selling costs as well as reaping well earned profit for taking the time to build your SET.

At the time I began this thread in the SSG, I had recently opened a store at eBay and began selling items online, some silver, some not. After making just a few one coin sales on eBay I began to think, "This isn't going to work. Postage costs are taking all my cash after fees." I was not eager to give up so much of my 'sales skin' unnecessarily.

I began to wonder why I was paying full postage on each coin sold: $2.60/coin (at the time) to ship them, with postage costs continuing to rise. Plus taking the time to deal with each coin sale one at a time, printer, tape, envelopes, delivery, other costs – there must be a better way.

Then I had a guy buy 10 different items at once ~ cost me $3.45 to ship everything ~ the rest of the saved shipping costs paid off some of the fees. 1 envelope; 1 label; 1 effort made to package it all up. Payday.

Something clicked.

I began thinking about selling a Proof and a couple or a few BUs with it ~ good savings on postage ~ kind of like Chris having to sell coins in 3-packs and 4-packs within the SSG to cover shipping costs. Then I thought about selling a POP Proof and some matching BU, maybe 10; even better savings on postage, and time. Then I conceived of the possibility of selling a whole set of POP Proofs along with 10 BU each ~ and then I had the **KING SET** revelation.

I began to write up an auction about it for eBay. From there I began to realize the actual value of what I possessed ~ not dollar-wise, yet ~ but relative to other SETs ~ could possibly be much greater than I had yet imagined, and a focus on SETs developed within me. Finally I needed to get something in writing and began a thread within the SSG, formalizing my ideas, which I have now taken and rewritten into this short valuable guide.

In fact, I began writing this information out in part as an effort to clarify and record a buying/selling strategy for myself ~ as I changed over from a buy/hold strategy. And I also wanted to make sure I offered such a rare SET for a fair price to all involved. And obviously, this is a great strategy to share with whomever could benefit from it as well, not just sellers but buyers looking for Complete SETs too.

My SET appeared flawless in my mind and I felt I needed to devise a system applicable to all SETs, because none currently existed, that would verify whether or not it was indeed as flawless as I imagined: Turns out it was. The more I considered what I had, the more all of this data just started falling into place.

I do not see this Guide as something I created or developed per se, but more as something that already always existed with regards to every SSG design ever issued, customizable to each and relevant to all, and that I was just able to bring it into focus, at a specific point in my stacking career, at a specific point in the POP issuance sequence, and I was able to share it with the SSG. I felt almost as if I had channeled this information as if this guide, for the most part, demanded that I bring it into existence.

After much thought, I'd concluded that selling SSG coins, otherwise known as Medallions, as SETs is the future ~ or at least it has a critical part to play in it. It appeared to me that SETs are the other half of Chris Duane's Micro-Mintage equation ~ and it is a natural outflow from what Chris and those of us who purchase his designs are doing. I see SSG SETs in the silver market as the equivalent of Golden Russian Faberge Eggs in the gold market. And I really don't believe anyone has contemplated this next level of investment performance before now in order to thoroughly map it out. The mapping is far from complete, but the groundwork has now been laid and amazing progress has been made. An entire new way of thinking about SSG coins is about to open up.

Thinking about groups of some of your own coins in SETs is an additional, strategic way to think about your coins when buying or selling them; or even just holding them for their Set VALUE. Some of us have been building SETs and truly hold more VALUE than we realize. People have loosely used the term 'Set' when describing different collections or groups of SSG coins, but now it can be defined much more precisely.

I had intended my SSG thread to be a work that attempted to define VALUE and why VALUE differences exist, why SET stackers should be concerned about them, and how we can use our knowledge to create more valuable SETs. Well, it turns out that the thread ended up being about RANKING VALUE. Not much explanation on Value itself, but this is the important information people will be turning to in order to determine Relative VALUE of one SET compared to another.

SET RULES AND THEORY

Here are some beginning ideas about SETS:

What *Flavor* of **POP Set** do you own? Or do you merely possess a **Collection**? Did you know: Your Pyramid Of Power silver stack actually has a specific TITLE now! Discover your Flavor in the following pages!

There are a few simple terms and ideas to learn and you can now talk about your sets in terms other POP stackers will instantly understand once they learn them as well. These terms can eventually be used to describe other sets too, as full Sets become complete over time. There will come a time when some of the coins we have been buying as parts of Sets become fully grouped together by stackers and some full Sets will begin to be offered. That is the concept I am working on. I believe that, in due time, full, Complete Sets will command hefty premiums over single coins sales, by leaps and bounds ~ we may in fact be at that point already. To me it's a no-brainer.

So, to begin a discussion of 'SETs' and to delineate SETs lingo, I present a number of novel ideas to consider. These are forward looking ideas defining what SETs are, and they can be used as guidelines in determining how pristine a SET is, any SSG SET, and where it ranks in desirability among potential moderately wealthy collectors or investors ~ those who simply want the Best Of The Best Available ~ and are happy to pay for it. If you want to sell a valuable SET for top dollar then this is a starting point for figuring TRUE VALUE for your SET ~ you have to start with a name for your SET that defines it specifically, a name defined by specific rules that apply to all SETs.

After that, we are finally able to competently move forward toward discovering said TRUE VALUE which, for larger SETs, may be far above what you might think it to be.

These SET guidelines, or RULES, were absolutely contemplated with the upper end of the SET market in mind, far from the day-to-day selling of onesy-twosy coins – although that was contemplated as well and its failure as a business model, at least to me, proved to be the beginning point of my contemplation – or else it could not have come about at all. But, all in all, it simply applies to all SETs, large and small.

Forward looking or not, I will begin to use many of the following terms from this point on in my SET auctions. You are welcome to use them as well, provided you use them accurately, as they have been laid out.

This is a value-measuring standard, a system for evaluating SSG coin collections and SETs, not based merely on spot price and specific coin rarity, that everyone will be able to use across the SSG market from this day forward. Will it apply to everyone? NO, not likely. But it will apply to many, many SSG stackers, once it us understood. And when the day comes that it applies to YOU, you will be grateful I took the time to share this here today. Guaranteed. But first let's take a look at the coins that make up the POP series of coins, then we will go over the terms.

PYRAMID OF POWER COINS AND MINTAGES

Let us now identify the coins that make up the Pyramid Of Power series. Chris Duane generally kept the first 20 of each coin he produced, those coins are included in the mintage numbers listed here. There are 14 different Proofs which are as follows, including mintages and year minted:

POP Proofs	Year	Mintages
1.) We Indoctrinate You	2015	260
2.) We Condemn You	2015	302
3.) We Fatten You	2015	315
4.) We Watch You	2015	315
5.) We Consume You	2015	375
6.) We Brutalize You	2015	350
7.) We Poison You	2015	325
8.) We Distract You (V1)	2015	355
9.) We Distract You (V2)	2015	530
10.) We Fool You	2015	600
11.) We Break You	2015	525
12.) We Break Them	2015	475
13.) We Rob You	2015	500
14.) We Own You	2015	650

The series also includes 14 BU (Brilliant Uncirculated) Pyramid Of Power coins, each BU matching a Proof, and the following are the statistics for those coins, including the year minted and their mintages:

POP BU	**Year**	**Mintages**
1.) We Indoctrinate You	2016	1400
2.) We Condemn You	2016	1400
3.) We Fatten You	2016	1300
4.) We Watch You	2016	1075
5.) We Consume You	2016	888
6.) We Brutalize You	2016	940
7.) We Poison You	2016	1075
8.) We Distract You (V1)	2016	980
9.) We Distract You (V2)	2016	785
10.) We Fool You	2016	805
11.) We Break You	2016	775
12.) We Break Them	2016	615
13.) We Rob You	2016	801
14.) We Own You	2016	819

Here are public domain pictures of each coin (in BU format):

1.) We Indoctrinate You

2.) We Condemn You

3.) We Fatten You

4.) We Watch You

5.) We Consume You

6.) We Brutalize You

7.) We Poison You

8.) We Distract You V1

9.) We Distract You V2

10.) We Fool You

11.) We Break You

12.) We Break Them

13.) We Rob You

14.) We Own You

2015 Proof Obverse

2016 BU Obverse

SETS DEFINED ~ BASIC SET RULES ~ 'DISCOVERING FLAVOR':

* COLLECTIONS VS SETS ~ HEAD AND HEARTS

* 1-11 different POP Proofs ~ **POP Proof Collection**, regardless which coins are missing (Collections are not Ranked but single POP Proofs accompanied by eligible BU are Ranked)

* 12-14 different POP Proofs ~ **POP Proof Set**, or **POP Set**

* Each **POP Set** has a *Head*, the Indoc Proof, and two *Hearts* among any of the rest of the Set ~ it can be missing two of the three and still be a Set, though incomplete; if all three are missing it becomes merely a POP Collection and falls short of a POP Set. Sets missing pieces have specific names, which can be thought of as *Flavors*:

- a **POP Set** missing only an Indoc Proof ~ **Headless POP Set, <u>or</u> POP Set Missing A Head**

- a **POP Set** missing only one Proof other than an Indoc ~ **POP Set Missing A Heart**

- a **POP Set** missing only two Proofs other than an Indoc ~ **Heartless Pop Set**

- a **POP Set** missing an Indoc and 1 other Proof ~ **Headless POP Set Missing A Heart, <u>or</u> POP Set Missing A Head Missing A Heart**

* SINGLE PROOF/BU SETS

** A single POP Proof offered with accompanying BU coins can be considered a Set of its own. Proof/BU Sets have different names depending upon how many BU are part of the Set; the exact names are variably customizable:*

- a single POP Proof with 1 or 2 same design BU ~ [POP Proof] Princess Set - (example: **Indoc Princess Set**, <u>or</u> **We Indoctrinate You Princess Set**)

- a single POP Proof with 3 or 4 same design BU ~ [POP Proof] Prince Set - (example: **Brutalize Prince Set**, <u>or</u> **We Brutalize You Prince Set**)

- a single POP Proof with 5 to 9 same design BU ~ [POP Proof] Queen Set - (example: **Poison Queen Set**, <u>or</u> **We Poison You Queen Set**)

- a single POP Proof with 10 to 19 same design BU ~ [POP Proof] King Set - (example: **Own You King Set**, <u>or</u> **We Own You King Set**)

- a single POP Proof with 20 or more same design BU - [POP Proof] Pope Set - (example: **Condemn Pope Set**, <u>or</u> **We Condemn You Pope Set**)

<u>* COMPLETE SETS</u>

** A **POP SET** offered with accompanying BU coins then becomes (POP [Type] Set); SETs missing a **Head** or **Heart(s)** must still have the required BU of the missing Proofs to be considered a Set/SET, though incomplete:*

- a **POP SET** with 1 or 2 same BU all designs ~ **POP Princess Set**

- a **POP SET** with 3 or 4 same BU all designs ~ **POP Prince Set**

- a **POP SET** with 5 to 9 same BU all designs ~ **POP QUEEN SET**

- a **POP SET** with 10 to 19 same BU all designs ~ **POP KING SET**

- a **POP SET** with 20 or more same BU all designs ~ **POP POPE SET**

- **QUEEN, KING** and **POPE POP SETs** are stellar accomplishments, inherently quite valuable, therefore noted with full capitalization of their SET name

* MULTIPLE SETS

* Some multiple **POP SETS** also have specific names as they increase in value exponentially when SETS are grouped together. However, the odds against many of these sets occurring, and then remaining together, are very great, thus their rarity is assured:*

- **2 POP QUEEN SETs** --> **POP KING SET** plus POP [Type] Set - (Princess or Prince, if more than 10 total of each BU in QUEEN SETs)

- **3 or more POP QUEEN SETs** --> **POP DIAMOND SET**

- a **POP DIAMOND SET** is also: a **POP KING SET** plus **POP QUEEN SET** plus POP [Type] SET (Princess or Prince, if more than 15 total of each BU in **QUEEN SETs**)

- **2 POP KING SETs** --> **POP CASTLE SET**
- **3 or more POP KING SETs** --> **POP EMPIRE SET**

- **2 POP POPE SETs** --> **POP CATHEDRAL SET**
- **3 or more POP POPE SETs** --> **POP VATICAN SET**

- the above sets are the ultimate SET goals for serious SET stackers ~ these SETs are the Crown Jewels of SSG Silver SETs ~ and will likely outperform any investment expectations, provided they are properly marketed as the incredibly rare, Complete SETs that they are

* WOUNDED SETS

** If SETs with 100 BU total or more are missing bits and pieces, they can still be considered a SET, called a **Wounded SET**, providing:*

- No more than 5 BU coins per/100 coins of SET are missing, and no more than 1 EA per design (5/100 allows for a slightly broader range of acceptably higher rated sets than 1/20 does; for over 100 BU, 1/20 applies as well)

- example: A **POP KING SET** missing 1 to 7 random BU coins, all different, becomes a **Wounded POP KING SET**

- example: A **POP KING SET** missing 2 to 7 random BU coins, at least two of one design, <u>or</u> more than 7 BU, becomes a **POP QUEEN SET**

- **example:** A **POP KING SET** missing only an Indoc Proof, as well as 1 to 7 ounces of BU, different designs, becomes a **Wounded, Headless POP KING SET**

- example: A **POP KING SET** missing only a Proof, other than an Indoc, as well as 1 to 7 ounces of BU, different designs, becomes a **Wounded POP KING SET Missing A Heart**

- example: A **POP KING SET** missing two Proofs other than an Indoc, as well as 1 to 7 ounces of BU, different designs, becomes a **Wounded, Heartless POP KING SET**

- a **Wounded POP KING SET** is basically a high-level **POP QUEEN SET**, or a **POP QUEEN SET with Distinction** ~ one on the precipice of becoming a true **POP KING SET** ~ similar distinctions can be made at every level of change

* PRIME SETS

** If SETs have consecutive serial numbered COAs then they can be considered to be **Prime**:*

- example: A **POP KING SET** with consecutive serial numbers becomes a **Prime POP KING SET**, and theoretically holds a measure of additional collector value over a similar, non-consecutive COA **POP KING SET**

* If anywhere from 1 up to 5 serial number gaps exist per 100 numbers then the Set can still be considered **Prime**, but it is now **Wounded** as well, but we will call it instead **2nd Prime** in order to avoid confusion:

- example: A **POP KING SET** with 5 BU serial numbers that are not consecutive with the others, becomes a **2nd Prime POP KING SET** (<u>or</u> a **Wounded Prime POP KING SET**)

- example: A **POP KING SET** missing an Indoc proof with 5 serial number gaps, becomes a **2nd Prime Headless POP KING SET** (<u>or</u> a **Wounded Prime Headless POP KING SET**)

- example: A **POP KING SET** with 5 serial number gaps, missing 3 random BU, different designs, becomes a **2nd Prime Wounded POP KING SET** (<u>or</u> a **Wounded Prime Wounded POP KING SET**)

* SET REPAIR ~ IMPROVING SET VALUE

* **Wounded SET**s are more severe than **Wounded** (or **2nd**) **Prime** is, one is missing actual physical parts of a SET, while the other is merely a matter of imperfections within a Complete SET. However, the great part about **Wounded SETs** is that they can be 'healed' simply by replacing the missing parts generally improving them to **2nd Prime** status. On the other hand, **2nd Prime** issues will likely take a bit of luck and/or hard work by the stacker to 'heal' properly, if possible; due to POP coin rarity it may be more or less impossible to 'heal' **2nd Prime** status issues.

So, what SET Label did I place upon the Pyramid Of Power Silver Shield Medallions that I stacked, you may be asking?

Simple: I stacked a **Prime POP CASTLE SET** plus a **Headless POP Set**, along with a small collection of **POP Proofs**. Some desirable Flavors for sure!

That should tell you almost to the coin the SET I was able to build.

Of course, I could look at it another way entirely: I can also accurately state that I built a **Prime POP POPE SET** plus a **POP Set** plus a **Headless POP Set**, as well as a small collection of **POP Proofs** ~ but that's not quite as tasty of a Flavor as the last! The important point here is that large SETs can be broken down and thought of in more ways than 1! And they can be sold, as SETs, anyway they are broken down.

As I've stated, I do not see this information on SETs as something that I created or developed, but more as something that was always already there with regards to every SSG design ever minted, customizable to each and relevant to all. I was just able to bring it into focus and capture it over a period of about a week or so, at a specific point in my stacking career, at a specific point in the POP series issuance, and I was able to share it with the SSG. And now it is available publicly as well.

Based upon my **Basic SET Rules** that I laid out earlier I was able to come up with the following 'predicted' Rank structure, after which I plugged numbers into each SET to determine the True Rank Structure:

PREDICTED RANKING FOR ALL POSSIBLE POP SETS
From Least to Most Desirable and Valuable:

1. [POP Proof] Princess Set

2. [POP Proof] Prince Set

3. [POP Proof] Queen Set

4. [POP Proof] King Set

5. [POP Proof] Pope Set

6. Headless POP Set Missing A Heart, or POP Set Missing A Head Missing A Heart

7. Headless POP Set, or POP Set Missing A Head

8. Heartless POP Set

9. POP Set Missing A Heart

10. POP Set

11. POP Princess Set RANKINGS ~ (Predicted) Lowest to Highest:

Headless, Wounded POP Princess Set Missing A Heart
Headless POP Princess Set Missing A Heart
Headless, Wounded POP Princess Set
Headless POP Princess Set
Heartless, Wounded POP Princess Set
Heartless POP Princess Set
Wounded POP Princess Set Missing A Heart
POP Princess Set Missing A Heart
2nd Prime Headless, Wounded POP Princess Set Missing A Heart
Prime Headless, Wounded POP Princess Set Missing A Heart
2nd Prime Headless, Wounded POP Princess Set
Prime Headless, Wounded POP Princess Set
2nd Prime Headless POP Princess Set
Prime Headless POP Princess Set
2nd Prime Heartless, Wounded POP Princess Set Missing A Heart
Prime Heartless, Wounded POP Princess Set Missing A Heart
2nd Prime Heartless, Wounded POP Princess Set
Prime Heartless, Wounded POP Princess Set
2nd Prime Heartless POP Princess Set
Prime Heartless POP Princess Set
2nd Prime Wounded POP Princess Set Missing A Heart
Prime Wounded POP Princess Set Missing A Heart
2nd Prime Wounded POP Princess Set
Prime Wounded POP Princess Set
POP Princess Set
2nd Prime POP Princess Set
Prime POP Princess Set

12. POP Prince Set RANKINGS ~ (Predicted) Lowest to Highest:

Headless, Wounded POP Prince Set Missing A Heart
Headless POP Prince Set Missing A Heart
Headless, Wounded POP Prince Set
Headless POP Prince Set
Heartless, Wounded POP Prince Set
Heartless POP Prince Set
Wounded POP Prince Set Missing A Heart
POP Prince Set Missing A Heart
2nd Prime Headless, Wounded POP Prince Set Missing A Heart
Prime Headless, Wounded POP Prince Set Missing A Heart
2nd Prime Headless, Wounded POP Prince Set
Prime Headless, Wounded POP Prince Set
2nd Prime Headless POP Prince Set
Prime Headless POP Prince Set
2nd Prime Heartless, Wounded POP Prince Set Missing A Heart
Prime Heartless, Wounded POP Prince Set Missing A Heart
2nd Prime Heartless, Wounded POP Prince Set
Prime Heartless, Wounded POP Prince Set
2nd Prime Heartless POP Prince Set
Prime Heartless POP Prince Set
2nd Prime Wounded POP Prince Set Missing A Heart
Prime Wounded POP Prince Set Missing A Heart
2nd Prime Wounded POP Prince Set
Prime Wounded POP Prince Set
POP Prince Set
2nd Prime POP Prince Set
Prime POP Prince Set

13. POP QUEEN SET RANKINGS ~ (Predicted) Lowest to Highest:

Headless, Wounded POP QUEEN SET Missing A Heart
Headless POP QUEEN SET Missing A Heart
Headless, Wounded POP QUEEN SET
Headless POP QUEEN SET
Heartless, Wounded POP QUEEN SET
Heartless POP QUEEN SET
Wounded POP QUEEN SET Missing A Heart
POP QUEEN SET Missing A Heart
2nd Prime Headless, Wounded POP QUEEN SET Missing A Heart
Prime Headless, Wounded POP QUEEN SET Missing A Heart
2nd Prime Headless, Wounded POP QUEEN SET
Prime Headless, Wounded POP QUEEN SET
2nd Prime Headless POP QUEEN SET
Prime Headless POP QUEEN SET
2nd Prime Heartless, Wounded POP QUEEN SET Missing A Heart
Prime Heartless, Wounded POP QUEEN SET Missing A Heart
2nd Prime Heartless, Wounded POP QUEEN SET
Prime Heartless, Wounded POP QUEEN SET
2nd Prime Heartless POP QUEEN SET
Prime Heartless POP QUEEN SET
2nd Prime Wounded POP QUEEN SET Missing A Heart
Prime Wounded POP QUEEN SET Missing A Heart
2nd Prime Wounded POP QUEEN SET
Prime Wounded POP QUEEN SET
POP QUEEN SET
2nd Prime POP QUEEN SET
Prime POP QUEEN SET

14. POP KING SET RANKINGS ~ (Predicted) Lowest to Highest:

Headless, Wounded POP KING SET Missing A Heart
Headless POP KING SET Missing A Heart
Headless, Wounded POP KING SET
Headless POP KING SET
Heartless, Wounded POP KING SET
Heartless POP KING SET
Wounded POP KING SET Missing A Heart
POP KING SET Missing A Heart
2nd Prime Headless, Wounded POP KING SET Missing A Heart
Prime Headless, Wounded POP KING SET Missing A Heart
2nd Prime Headless, Wounded POP KING SET
Prime Headless, Wounded POP KING SET
2nd Prime Headless POP KING SET
Prime Headless POP KING SET
2nd Prime Heartless, Wounded POP KING SET Missing A Heart
Prime Heartless, Wounded POP KING SET Missing A Heart
2nd Prime Heartless, Wounded POP KING SET
Prime Heartless, Wounded POP KING SET
2nd Prime Heartless POP KING SET
Prime Heartless POP KING SET
2nd Prime Wounded POP KING SET Missing A Heart
Prime Wounded POP KING SET Missing A Heart
2nd Prime Wounded POP KING SET
Prime Wounded POP KING SET
POP KING SET
2nd Prime POP KING SET
Prime POP KING SET

15. POP POPE SET RANKINGS ~ (Predicted) Lowest to Highest:

Headless, Wounded POP POPE SET Missing A Heart
Headless POP POPE SET Missing A Heart
Headless, Wounded POP POPE SET
Headless POP POPE SET
Heartless, Wounded POP POPE SET
Heartless POP POPE SET
Wounded POP POPE SET Missing A Heart
POP POPE SET Missing A Heart
2nd Prime Headless, Wounded POP POPE SET Missing A Heart
Prime Headless, Wounded POP POPE SET Missing A Heart
2nd Prime Headless, Wounded POP POPE SET
Prime Headless, Wounded POP POPE SET
2nd Prime Headless POP POPE SET
Prime Headless POP POPE SET
2nd Prime Heartless, Wounded POP POPE SET Missing A Heart
Prime Heartless, Wounded POP POPE SET Missing A Heart
2nd Prime Heartless, Wounded POP POPE SET
Prime Heartless, Wounded POP POPE SET
2nd Prime Heartless POP POPE SET
Prime Heartless POP POPE SET
2nd Prime Wounded POP POPE SET Missing A Heart
Prime Wounded POP POPE SET Missing A Heart
2nd Prime Wounded POP POPE SET
Prime Wounded POP POPE SET
POP POPE SET
2nd Prime POP POPE SET
Prime POP POPE SET

16. POP DIAMOND SET RANKINGS ~ (Predicted) Lowest to Highest:

Headless, Wounded POP DIAMOND SET Missing A Heart
Headless POP DIAMOND SET Missing A Heart
Headless, Wounded POP DIAMOND SET
Headless POP DIAMOND SET
Heartless, Wounded POP DIAMOND SET
Heartless POP DIAMOND SET
Wounded POP DIAMOND SET Missing A Heart
POP DIAMOND SET Missing A Heart
2nd Prime Headless, Wounded POP DIAMOND SET Missing A Heart
Prime Headless, Wounded POP DIAMOND SET Missing A Heart
2nd Prime Headless, Wounded POP DIAMOND SET
Prime Headless, Wounded POP DIAMOND SET
2nd Prime Headless POP DIAMOND SET
Prime Headless POP DIAMOND SET
2nd Prime Heartless, Wounded POP DIAMOND SET Missing A Heart
Prime Heartless, Wounded POP DIAMOND SET Missing A Heart
2nd Prime Heartless, Wounded POP DIAMOND SET
Prime Heartless, Wounded POP DIAMOND SET
2nd Prime Heartless POP DIAMOND SET
Prime Heartless POP DIAMOND SET
2nd Prime Wounded POP DIAMOND SET Missing A Heart
Prime Wounded POP DIAMOND SET Missing A Heart
2nd Prime Wounded POP DIAMOND SET
Prime Wounded POP DIAMOND SET
POP DIAMOND SET
2nd Prime POP DIAMOND SET
Prime POP DIAMOND SET

17. POP CASTLE SET RANKINGS ~ (Predicted) Lowest to Highest:

Headless, Wounded POP CASTLE SET Missing A Heart
Headless POP CASTLE SET Missing A Heart
Headless, Wounded POP CASTLE SET
Headless POP CASTLE SET
Heartless, Wounded POP CASTLE SET
Heartless POP CASTLE SET
Wounded POP CASTLE SET Missing A Heart
POP CASTLE SET Missing A Heart
2nd Prime Headless, Wounded POP CASTLE SET Missing A Heart
Prime Headless, Wounded POP CASTLE SET Missing A Heart
2nd Prime Headless, Wounded POP CASTLE SET
Prime Headless, Wounded POP CASTLE SET
2nd Prime Headless POP CASTLE SET
Prime Headless POP CASTLE SET
2nd Prime Heartless, Wounded POP CASTLE SET Missing A Heart
Prime Heartless, Wounded POP CASTLE SET Missing A Heart
2nd Prime Heartless, Wounded POP CASTLE SET
Prime Heartless, Wounded POP CASTLE SET
2nd Prime Heartless POP CASTLE SET
Prime Heartless POP CASTLE SET
2nd Prime Wounded POP CASTLE SET Missing A Heart
Prime Wounded POP CASTLE SET Missing A Heart
2nd Prime Wounded POP CASTLE SET
Prime Wounded POP CASTLE SET
POP CASTLE SET
2nd Prime POP CASTLE SET
Prime POP CASTLE SET

18. POP EMPIRE SET RANKINGS ~ (Predicted) Lowest to Highest:

Headless, Wounded POP EMPIRE SET Missing A Heart
Headless POP EMPIRE SET Missing A Heart
Headless, Wounded POP EMPIRE SET
Headless POP EMPIRE SET
Heartless, Wounded POP EMPIRE SET
Heartless POP EMPIRE SET
Wounded POP EMPIRE SET Missing A Heart
POP EMPIRE SET Missing A Heart
2nd Prime Headless, Wounded POP EMPIRE SET Missing A Heart
Prime Headless, Wounded POP EMPIRE SET Missing A Heart
2nd Prime Headless, Wounded POP EMPIRE SET
Prime Headless, Wounded POP EMPIRE SET
2nd Prime Headless POP EMPIRE SET
Prime Headless POP EMPIRE SET
2nd Prime Heartless, Wounded POP EMPIRE SET Missing A Heart
Prime Heartless, Wounded POP EMPIRE SET Missing A Heart
2nd Prime Heartless, Wounded POP EMPIRE SET
Prime Heartless, Wounded POP EMPIRE SET
2nd Prime Heartless POP EMPIRE SET
Prime Heartless POP EMPIRE SET
2nd Prime Wounded POP EMPIRE SET Missing A Heart
Prime Wounded POP EMPIRE SET Missing A Heart
2nd Prime Wounded POP EMPIRE SET
Prime Wounded POP EMPIRE SET
POP EMPIRE SET
2nd Prime POP EMPIRE SET
Prime POP EMPIRE SET

19. POP CATHEDRAL SET RANKINGS ~ (Predicted) Lowest to Highest:

Headless, Wounded POP CATHEDRAL SET Missing A Heart
Headless POP CATHEDRAL SET Missing A Heart
Headless, Wounded POP CATHEDRAL SET
Headless POP CATHEDRAL SET
Heartless, Wounded POP CATHEDRAL SET
Heartless POP CATHEDRAL SET
Wounded POP CATHEDRAL SET Missing A Heart
POP CATHEDRAL SET Missing A Heart
2nd Prime Headless, Wounded POP CATHEDRAL SET Missing A Heart
Prime Headless, Wounded POP CATHEDRAL SET Missing A Heart
2nd Prime Headless, Wounded POP CATHEDRAL SET
Prime Headless, Wounded POP CATHEDRAL SET
2nd Prime Headless POP CATHEDRAL SET
Prime Headless POP CATHEDRAL SET
2nd Prime Heartless, Wounded POP CATHEDRAL SET Missing A Heart
Prime Heartless, Wounded POP CATHEDRAL SET Missing A Heart
2nd Prime Heartless, Wounded POP CATHEDRAL SET
Prime Heartless, Wounded POP CATHEDRAL SET
2nd Prime Heartless POP CATHEDRAL SET
Prime Heartless POP CATHEDRAL SET
2nd Prime Wounded POP CATHEDRAL SET Missing A Heart
Prime Wounded POP CATHEDRAL SET Missing A Heart
2nd Prime Wounded POP CATHEDRAL SET
Prime Wounded POP CATHEDRAL SET
POP CATHEDRAL SET
2nd Prime POP CATHEDRAL SET
Prime POP CATHEDRAL SET

20. POP VATICAN SET RANKINGS ~ (Predicted) Lowest to Highest:

Headless, Wounded POP VATICAN SET Missing A Heart
Headless POP VATICAN SET Missing A Heart
Headless, Wounded POP VATICAN SET
Headless POP VATICAN SET
Heartless, Wounded POP VATICAN SET
Heartless POP VATICAN SET
Wounded POP VATICAN SET Missing A Heart
POP VATICAN SET Missing A Heart
2nd Prime Headless, Wounded POP VATICAN SET Missing A Heart
Prime Headless, Wounded POP VATICAN SET Missing A Heart
2nd Prime Headless, Wounded POP VATICAN SET
Prime Headless, Wounded POP VATICAN SET
2nd Prime Headless POP VATICAN SET
Prime Headless POP VATICAN SET
2nd Prime Heartless, Wounded POP VATICAN SET Missing A Heart
Prime Heartless, Wounded POP VATICAN SET Missing A Heart
2nd Prime Heartless, Wounded POP VATICAN SET
Prime Heartless, Wounded POP VATICAN SET
2nd Prime Heartless POP VATICAN SET
Prime Heartless POP VATICAN SET
2nd Prime Wounded POP VATICAN SET Missing A Heart
Prime Wounded POP VATICAN SET Missing A Heart
2nd Prime Wounded POP VATICAN SET
Prime Wounded POP VATICAN SET
POP VATICAN SET
2nd Prime POP VATICAN SET

** Prime POP VATICAN SET **

THIS IS THE TOP SET POSSIBLE ~ IT'S VALUE IS BEYOND OTHERWISE LOGICAL COMPREHENSION ~ compared to ounces of silver involved in this highly desirable and **PINNACLE ~SSG POP SET~.**

At this point we have a list of all possible SETs. But this is only a list based upon my intuitive presumption of value and, as stated, my **Basic SET Rules**. There no numerical values yet included within this list. But, we will now define numerical values for each SET listed. These values will be based upon positives and negatives inherent within each specific SET being defined. THESE ARE NOT DOLLAR VALUES ~ but dollars (or any other currency) can and will be based upon these numerical values in due time.

Here's what I've come up with. Each Set receives a **Point Rating** based upon its **Attributes**. I've rated each **Attribute** according to the *Severity Of Its State* (missing coins, COAs, etc.) and each gets a score, shown below. Each level from SET Levels 11-19 shows a number in bold indicating **Start Points**, and each level starts with 1,000 points more than the last level. Choose your level, check your **Start Points**, then choose your **Set Name** based upon the **Attributes** of your SET, the one that accurately describes the SET you own. Then identify the corresponding **Attributes** on the following page and add or subtract the number next to the **Attribute** from your **Start Points** to find your score! It's that simple. Max Points per level is 1,000, the Perfect Set for that level. You can do it yourself, but I have already plugged the numbers in. Well, I kind of had to. I had to plug numbers in and modify them until I found the correct ones – the first ones didn't work. But now it works AMAZING!

Every SET rating begins with adding 650 Points to the **Start Points** for your Level ~ from there points can go up and/or down. If your SET is Wounded, subtract 100 points, as well as 10 additional points for each Missing BU; if not move on. If you're **Headless, Heartless** or **Missing A Heart**, subtract the appropriate points. If your SET is **2nd Prime** you can add 100 points, if it's **Prime** you can add a full 250 points. The second and third Finest SETs receive an additional 75 Bonus Points for <u>ACHIEVEMENT</u> ~ they have NO Missing Proofs or BU, they only possess serial number discrepancies. Truly some great stacking deserving of a reward! The Finest SET of the Level receives a full 100 Bonus Points for **PERFECTION** and achieves a Perfect Score of 1,000 points for the level ~ which is why each level begins 1,000 points higher than the last level. Epic Stacking for sure!

ATTRIBUTES ~
NUMERICAL VALUES OF POTENTIAL SET STATES:

+650   SET (full)
-100   Wounded
+100   2nd Prime
+250   Prime

MEDALLION POINTS:

-200   Heart Coin
-350   Heartless
-375   Indoc
+/-10   Per BU

ADDITIONAL POTENTIAL DINGS:

-100   Proof Missing COA
-5   BU Missing COA
N/A   COA Missing Proof ~ Get A New Proof!

As an example I've taken the predicted **POP KING SET** rankings and plugged numbers for their corresponding **Attributes** into them on the following page.

<u>14. (~~PREDICTED~~) POP KING SETs RANKINGS ~</u>
<u>Lowest to Highest (Start Points 13000+/-):</u>

<u>POINTS / SET NAME</u>

13025- Wounded, Headless POP KING Missing A Heart
13125   Headless POP KING Missing A Heart
13175- Wounded, Headless POP KING
13275   Headless POP KING
13200- Wounded, Heartless POP KING
13300   Heartless POP KING
13350- Wounded POP KING Missing A Heart
13450   POP KING Missing A Heart

13075- 2nd Prime Wounded, Headless POP KING Missing A Heart
13225- Prime Wounded, Headless POP KING Missing A Heart
13175   2nd Prime Headless POP KING Missing A Heart
13350   Prime Headless POP KING Missing A Heart
13275- 2nd Prime Wounded, Headless POP KING
13425- Prime Wounded, Headless POP KING
13375   2nd Prime Headless POP KING
13525   Prime Headless POP KING

13300- 2nd Prime Wounded, Heartless POP KING
13450- Prime Wounded, Heartless POP KING
13400   2nd Prime Heartless POP KING
13550   Prime Heartless POP KING

13450- 2nd Prime Wounded POP KING Missing A Heart
13600- Prime Wounded POP KING Missing A Heart
13550   2nd Prime POP KING Missing A Heart
13600   Prime POP KING Missing A Heart

13650- 2nd Prime Wounded POP KING
13800- Prime Wounded POP KING

13725+ POP KING
13825+ 2nd Prime POP KING

14000++ Prime POP KING

ANNOTATIONS:
(from previous page, the next page and also in Final Rank Structure):

- => These RANKS includes an unknown Variable: Reduce the number by 10 points further per Missing BU, up to 7 pieces, for an accurate rating

+ => These RANKS have earned and include a bonus of 75 points for having no missing Proofs or BU, only serial number discrepancies

++ => This SET has earned an included bonus of 100 points for
PERFECTION

All right, so now we're really starting to get down to the nitty-gritty with regards to specific values placed on specific SETs.

Notice that the point levels listed above correspond very nicely to the order I chose for my 'Predicted List.' You can see the numbers gradually increasing as you go down the page, although not all of the numbers line up perfectly, but that's fine, they weren't meant to, it was an estimation, a prediction ~ the numbers are supposed to speak for themselves after all. But now is when the details of the **Attributes** of each SET begin to become evident.

Ultimately we are looking for the precise order from Lowest to Highest, so I must rearrange some SET names according to their point values yet. ~/~ I've now done that and my results are below:

14. (ACTUAL) POP KING SETs RANKINGS ~
Lowest to Highest (Start Points 13000+/-):

POINTS / SET NAME

13025- Wounded, Headless POP KING Missing A Heart
13075- 2nd Prime Wounded, Headless POP KING Missing A Heart
13125   Headless POP KING Missing A Heart
13175- Wounded, Headless POP KING
13175   2nd Prime Headless POP KING Missing A Heart

13200- Wounded, Heartless POP KING
13225- Prime Wounded, Headless POP KING Missing A Heart
13275- 2nd Prime Wounded, Headless POP KING
13275   Headless POP KING

13300- 2nd Prime Wounded, Heartless POP KING
13300   Heartless POP KING
13350- Wounded POP KING Missing A Heart
13350   Prime Headless POP KING Missing A Heart
13375   2nd Prime Headless POP KING

13400   2nd Prime Heartless POP KING
13425- Prime Wounded, Headless POP KING
13450- Prime Wounded, Heartless POP KING
13450- 2nd Prime Wounded POP KING Missing A Heart
13450   POP KING Missing A Heart

13525   Prime Headless POP KING
13550   Prime Heartless POP KING
13550   2nd Prime POP KING Missing A Heart

13600- Prime Wounded POP KING Missing A Heart
13600   Prime POP KING Missing A Heart
13650- 2nd Prime Wounded POP KING

13725+ POP KING
13800- Prime Wounded POP KING
13825+ 2nd Prime POP KING

14000++   Prime POP KING

FINAL VALUES AND PERMANENT RANK STRUCTURE:

Okay, now that the above results are finalized the following section reflects the values, or the RANKS, now assessed on ALL SSG POP SETS in relation to all other POP SETS.

POINT VALUES NOW ASSESSED ON SSG POP Sets:

200   1. [POP (single) Proof] Princess Set ~ with BU

400   2. [POP (single) Proof] Prince Set ~ with BU

700   3. [POP (single) Proof] Queen Set ~ with BU

950   4. [POP (single) Proof] King Set ~ with BU

1250   5. [POP (single) Proof] Pope Set ~ with BU

1425   6. Headless POP Set Missing A Heart (or: POP Set Missing A Head Missing A Heart) ~ 12 Proofs, no BU

1625   7. Headless POP Set (or, POP Set Missing A Head) ~ 13 Proofs, no BU

1650   8. Heartless POP Set ~ 12 Proofs, no BU

1800   9. POP Set Missing A Heart ~ 13 Proofs, no BU

2000   10. POP Set ~ 14 Proofs, no BU

What follows now is the complete RANK structure including numerical values for each **POP SET**.

11. POP Princess Sets RANKINGS ~
Lowest to Highest (Start Points 10000+/-):

POINTS / SET NAME

10025- Wounded, Headless POP Princess Missing A Heart
10075- 2nd Prime Wounded, Headless POP Princess Missing A Heart
10125   Headless POP Princess Missing A Heart
10175- Wounded, Headless POP Princess
10175   2nd Prime Headless POP Princess Missing A Heart

10200- Wounded, Heartless POP Princess
10225- Prime Wounded, Headless POP Princess Missing A Heart
10275- 2nd Prime Wounded, Headless POP Princess
10275   Headless POP Princess

10300- 2nd Prime Wounded, Heartless POP Princess
10300   Heartless POP Princess
10350- Wounded POP Princess Missing A Heart
10350   Prime Headless POP Princess Missing A Heart
10375   2nd Prime Headless POP Princess

10400   2nd Prime Heartless POP Princess
10425- Prime Wounded, Headless POP Princess
10450- Prime Wounded, Heartless POP Princess
10450- 2nd Prime Wounded POP Princess Missing A Heart
10450   POP Princess Missing A Heart

10525   Prime Headless POP Princess
10550   Prime Heartless POP Princess
10550   2nd Prime POP Princess Missing A Heart

10600- Prime Wounded POP Princess Missing A Heart
10600   Prime POP Princess Missing A Heart
10650- 2nd Prime Wounded POP Princess

10725+ POP Princess
10800- Prime Wounded POP Princess
10825+ 2nd Prime POP Princess

11000++ Prime POP Princess

12. POP Prince Sets RANKINGS ~
Lowest to Highest (Start Points 11000+/-):

POINTS / SET NAME

11025- Wounded, Headless POP Prince Missing A Heart
11075- 2nd Prime Wounded, Headless POP Prince Missing A Heart
11125   Headless POP Prince Missing A Heart
11175- Wounded, Headless POP Prince
11175   2nd Prime Headless POP Prince Missing A Heart

11200- Wounded, Heartless POP Prince
11225- Prime Wounded, Headless POP Prince Missing A Heart
11275- 2nd Prime Wounded, Headless POP Prince
11275   Headless POP Prince

11300- 2nd Prime Wounded, Heartless POP Prince
11300   Heartless POP Prince
11350- Wounded POP Prince Missing A Heart
11350   Prime Headless POP Prince Missing A Heart
11375   2nd Prime Headless POP Prince

11400   2nd Prime Heartless POP Prince
11425- Prime Wounded, Headless POP Prince
11450- Prime Wounded, Heartless POP Prince
11450- 2nd Prime Wounded POP Prince Missing A Heart
11450   POP Prince Missing A Heart

11525   Prime Headless POP Prince
11550   Prime Heartless POP Prince
11550   2nd Prime POP Prince Missing A Heart

11600- Prime Wounded POP Prince Missing A Heart
11600   Prime POP Prince Missing A Heart
11650- 2nd Prime Wounded POP Prince

11725+ POP Prince
11800- Prime Wounded POP Prince
11825+ 2nd Prime POP Prince

12000++ Prime POP Prince

13. POP QUEEN SETs RANKINGS ~
Lowest to Highest (Start Points 12000+/-):

POINTS / SET NAME

12025- Wounded, Headless POP QUEEN Missing A Heart
12075- 2nd Prime Wounded, Headless POP QUEEN Missing A Heart
12125   Headless POP QUEEN Missing A Heart
12175- Wounded, Headless POP QUEEN
12175   2nd Prime Headless POP QUEEN Missing A Heart

12200- Wounded, Heartless POP QUEEN
12225- Prime Wounded, Headless POP QUEEN Missing A Heart
12275- 2nd Prime Wounded, Headless POP QUEEN
12275   Headless POP QUEEN

12300- 2nd Prime Wounded, Heartless POP QUEEN
12300   Heartless POP QUEEN
12350- Wounded POP QUEEN Missing A Heart
12350   Prime Headless POP QUEEN Missing A Heart
12375   2nd Prime Headless POP QUEEN

12400   2nd Prime Heartless POP QUEEN
12425- Prime Wounded, Headless POP QUEEN
12450- Prime Wounded, Heartless POP QUEEN
12450- 2nd Prime Wounded POP QUEEN Missing A Heart
12450   POP QUEEN Missing A Heart

12525   Prime Headless POP QUEEN
12550   Prime Heartless POP QUEEN
12550   2nd Prime POP QUEEN Missing A Heart

12600- Prime Wounded POP QUEEN Missing A Heart
12600   Prime POP QUEEN Missing A Heart
12650- 2nd Prime Wounded POP QUEEN

12725+ POP QUEEN
12800- Prime Wounded POP QUEEN
12825+ 2nd Prime POP QUEEN

13000++   Prime POP QUEEN

14. POP KING SETs RANKINGS ~
Lowest to Highest (Start Points 13000+/-):

POINTS / SET NAME

13025- Wounded, Headless POP KING Missing A Heart
13075- 2nd Prime Wounded, Headless POP KING Missing A Heart
13125   Headless POP KING Missing A Heart
13175- Wounded, Headless POP KING
13175   2nd Prime Headless POP KING Missing A Heart

13200- Wounded, Heartless POP KING
13225- Prime Wounded, Headless POP KING Missing A Heart
13275- 2nd Prime Wounded, Headless POP KING
13275   Headless POP KING

13300- 2nd Prime Wounded, Heartless POP KING
13300   Heartless POP KING
13350- Wounded POP KING Missing A Heart
13350   Prime Headless POP KING Missing A Heart
13375   2nd Prime Headless POP KING

13400   2nd Prime Heartless POP KING
13425- Prime Wounded, Headless POP KING
13450- Prime Wounded, Heartless POP KING
13450- 2nd Prime Wounded POP KING Missing A Heart
13450   POP KING Missing A Heart

13525   Prime Headless POP KING
13550   Prime Heartless POP KING
13550   2nd Prime POP KING Missing A Heart

13600- Prime Wounded POP KING Missing A Heart
13600   Prime POP KING Missing A Heart
13650- 2nd Prime Wounded POP KING

13725+ POP KING
13800- Prime Wounded POP KING
13825+ 2nd Prime POP KING

14000++   Prime POP KING

15. POP POPE SETs RANKINGS ~
Lowest to Highest (Start Points 14000+/-):

POINTS / SET NAME

14025- Wounded, Headless POP POPE Missing A Heart
14075- 2nd Prime Wounded, Headless POP POPE Missing A Heart
14125   Headless POP POPE Missing A Heart
14175- Wounded, Headless POP POPE
14175   2nd Prime Headless POP POPE Missing A Heart

14200- Wounded, Heartless POP POPE
14225- Prime Wounded, Headless POP POPE Missing A Heart
14275- 2nd Prime Wounded, Headless POP POPE
14275   Headless POP POPE

14300- 2nd Prime Wounded, Heartless POP POPE
14300   Heartless POP POPE
14350- Wounded POP POPE Missing A Heart
14350   Prime Headless POP POPE Missing A Heart
14375   2nd Prime Headless POP POPE

14400   2nd Prime Heartless POP POPE
14425- Prime Wounded, Headless POP POPE
14450- Prime Wounded, Heartless POP POPE
14450- 2nd Prime Wounded POP POPE Missing A Heart
14450   POP POPE Missing A Heart

14525   Prime Headless POP POPE
14550   Prime Heartless POP POPE
14550   2nd Prime POP POPE Missing A Heart

14600- Prime Wounded POP POPE Missing A Heart
14600   Prime POP POPE Missing A Heart
14650- 2nd Prime Wounded POP POPE

14725+ POP POPE
14800- Prime Wounded POP POPE
14825+ 2nd Prime POP POPE

15000++   Prime POP POPE

16. POP DIAMOND SETs RANKINGS ~
Lowest to Highest (Start Points 15000+/-):

POINTS / SET NAME

15025- Wounded, Headless POP DIAMOND Missing A Heart
15075- 2nd Prime Wounded, Headless POP DIAMOND Missing A Heart
15125   Headless POP DIAMOND Missing A Heart
15175- Wounded, Headless POP DIAMOND
15175   2nd Prime Headless POP DIAMOND Missing A Heart

15200- Wounded, Heartless POP DIAMOND
15225- Prime Wounded, Headless POP DIAMOND Missing A Heart
15275- 2nd Prime Wounded, Headless POP DIAMOND
15275   Headless POP DIAMOND

15300- 2nd Prime Wounded, Heartless POP DIAMOND
15300   Heartless POP DIAMOND
15350- Wounded POP DIAMOND Missing A Heart
15350   Prime Headless POP DIAMOND Missing A Heart
15375   2nd Prime Headless POP DIAMOND

15400   2nd Prime Heartless POP DIAMOND
15425- Prime Wounded, Headless POP DIAMOND
15450- Prime Wounded, Heartless POP DIAMOND
15450- 2nd Prime Wounded POP DIAMOND Missing A Heart
15450   POP DIAMOND Missing A Heart

15525   Prime Headless POP DIAMOND
15550   Prime Heartless POP DIAMOND
15550   2nd Prime POP DIAMOND Missing A Heart

15600- Prime Wounded POP DIAMOND Missing A Heart
15600   Prime POP DIAMOND Missing A Heart
15650- 2nd Prime Wounded POP DIAMOND

15725+ POP DIAMOND
15800- Prime Wounded POP DIAMOND
15825+ 2nd Prime POP DIAMOND

16000++   Prime POP DIAMOND

17. POP CASTLE SETs RANKINGS ~
Lowest to Highest (Start Points 16000+/-):

POINTS / SET NAME

16025- Wounded, Headless POP CASTLE Missing A Heart
16075- 2nd Prime Wounded, Headless POP CASTLE Missing A Heart
16125   Headless POP CASTLE Missing A Heart
16175- Wounded, Headless POP CASTLE
16175   2nd Prime Headless POP CASTLE Missing A Heart

16200- Wounded, Heartless POP CASTLE
16225- Prime Wounded, Headless POP CASTLE Missing A Heart
16275- 2nd Prime Wounded, Headless POP CASTLE
16275   Headless POP CASTLE

16300- 2nd Prime Wounded, Heartless POP CASTLE
16300   Heartless POP CASTLE
16350- Wounded POP CASTLE Missing A Heart
16350   Prime Headless POP CASTLE Missing A Heart
16375   2nd Prime Headless POP CASTLE

16400   2nd Prime Heartless POP CASTLE
16425- Prime Wounded, Headless POP CASTLE
16450- Prime Wounded, Heartless POP CASTLE
16450- 2nd Prime Wounded POP CASTLE Missing A Heart
16450   POP CASTLE Missing A Heart

16525   Prime Headless POP CASTLE
16550   Prime Heartless POP CASTLE
16550   2nd Prime POP CASTLE Missing A Heart

16600- Prime Wounded POP CASTLE Missing A Heart
16600   Prime POP CASTLE Missing A Heart
16650- 2nd Prime Wounded POP CASTLE

16725+ POP CASTLE
16800- Prime Wounded POP CASTLE
16825+ 2nd Prime POP CASTLE

17000++   Prime POP CASTLE

18. POP EMPIRE SETs RANKINGS ~
Lowest to Highest (Start Points 17000+/-):

POINTS / SET NAME

17025- Wounded, Headless POP EMPIRE Missing A Heart
17075- 2nd Prime Wounded, Headless POP EMPIRE Missing A Heart
17125 Headless POP EMPIRE Missing A Heart
17175- Wounded, Headless POP EMPIRE
17175 2nd Prime Headless POP EMPIRE Missing A Heart

17200- Wounded, Heartless POP EMPIRE
17225- Prime Wounded, Headless POP EMPIRE Missing A Heart
17275- 2nd Prime Wounded, Headless POP EMPIRE
17275 Headless POP EMPIRE

17300- 2nd Prime Wounded, Heartless POP EMPIRE
17300 Heartless POP EMPIRE
17350- Wounded POP EMPIRE Missing A Heart
17350 Prime Headless POP EMPIRE Missing A Heart
17375 2nd Prime Headless POP EMPIRE

17400 2nd Prime Heartless POP EMPIRE
17425- Prime Wounded, Headless POP EMPIRE
17450- Prime Wounded, Heartless POP EMPIRE
17450- 2nd Prime Wounded POP EMPIRE Missing A Heart
17450 POP EMPIRE Missing A Heart

17525 Prime Headless POP EMPIRE
17550 Prime Heartless POP EMPIRE
17550 2nd Prime POP EMPIRE Missing A Heart

17600- Prime Wounded POP EMPIRE Missing A Heart
17600 Prime POP EMPIRE Missing A Heart
17650- 2nd Prime Wounded POP EMPIRE

17725+ POP EMPIRE
17800- Prime Wounded POP EMPIRE
17825+ 2nd Prime POP EMPIRE

18000++ Prime POP EMPIRE

19. POP CATHEDRAL SETs RANKINGS ~
Lowest to Highest (Start Points 18000+/-):

POINTS / SET NAME

18025- Wounded, Headless POP CATHEDRAL Missing A Heart
18075- 2nd Prime Wounded, Headless POP CATHEDRAL Missing A Heart
18125   Headless POP CATHEDRAL Missing A Heart
18175- Wounded, Headless POP CATHEDRAL
18175   2nd Prime Headless POP CATHEDRAL Missing A Heart

18200- Wounded, Heartless POP CATHEDRAL
18225- Prime Wounded, Headless POP CATHEDRAL Missing A Heart
18275- 2nd Prime Wounded, Headless POP CATHEDRAL
18275   Headless POP CATHEDRAL

18300- 2nd Prime Wounded, Heartless POP CATHEDRAL
18300   Heartless POP CATHEDRAL
18350- Wounded POP CATHEDRAL Missing A Heart
18350   Prime Headless POP CATHEDRAL Missing A Heart
18375   2nd Prime Headless POP CATHEDRAL

18400   2nd Prime Heartless POP CATHEDRAL
18425- Prime Wounded, Headless POP CATHEDRAL
18450- Prime Wounded, Heartless POP CATHEDRAL
18450- 2nd Prime Wounded POP CATHEDRAL Missing A Heart
18450   POP CATHEDRAL Missing A Heart

18525   Prime Headless POP CATHEDRAL
18550   Prime Heartless POP CATHEDRAL
18550   2nd Prime POP CATHEDRAL Missing A Heart

18600- Prime Wounded POP CATHEDRAL Missing A Heart
18600   Prime POP CATHEDRAL Missing A Heart
18650- 2nd Prime Wounded POP CATHEDRAL

18725+ POP CATHEDRAL
18800- Prime Wounded POP CATHEDRAL
18825+ 2nd Prime POP CATHEDRAL

19000++   Prime POP CATHEDRAL

20. POP VATICAN SETs RANKINGS ~
Lowest to Highest (Start Points 19000+/-):

POINTS / SET NAME

19025- Wounded, Headless POP VATICAN Missing A Heart
19075- 2nd Prime Wounded, Headless POP VATICAN Missing A Heart
19125   Headless POP VATICAN Missing A Heart
19175- Wounded, Headless POP VATICAN
19175   2nd Prime Headless POP VATICAN Missing A Heart

19200- Wounded, Heartless POP VATICAN
19225- Prime Wounded, Headless POP VATICAN Missing A Heart
19275- 2nd Prime Wounded, Headless POP VATICAN
19275   Headless POP VATICAN

19300- 2nd Prime Wounded, Heartless POP VATICAN
19300   Heartless POP VATICAN
19350- Wounded POP VATICAN Missing A Heart
19350   Prime Headless POP VATICAN Missing A Heart
19375   2nd Prime Headless POP VATICAN

19400   2nd Prime Heartless POP VATICAN
19425- Prime Wounded, Headless POP VATICAN
19450- Prime Wounded, Heartless POP VATICAN
19450- 2nd Prime Wounded POP VATICAN Missing A Heart
19450   POP VATICAN Missing A Heart

19525   Prime Headless POP VATICAN
19550   Prime Heartless POP VATICAN
19550   2nd Prime POP VATICAN Missing A Heart

19600- Prime Wounded POP VATICAN Missing A Heart
19600   Prime POP VATICAN Missing A Heart
19650- 2nd Prime Wounded POP VATICAN

19725+ POP VATICAN
19800- Prime Wounded POP VATICAN
19825+ 2nd Prime POP VATICAN

20000++   Prime POP VATICAN

Once again:

The **Prime POP VATICAN** is the *TOP SET POSSIBLE* and theoretically holds a **VALUE BEYOND OTHERWISE LOGICAL COMPREHENSION** ~ compared to ounces of silver involved in this highly rare and desirable, and possibly non-existent, <u>PINNACLE</u> ~ SSG Pyramid Of Power SET ~.

ESTIMATED SILVER OUNCES PER SET:

The following section indicates how many ounces of silver are estimated to be included in each SET. Multiply these numbers as needed to calculate silver ounces required for the higher, **Multiple SETs** Ranks (**Headless, Heartless and Wounded SETs** are considered and included in these calculations):

POP Princess Set
* 12-14 Proofs ~ 1 or 2 of each BU (14-28 BU)

POP Prince Set
* 12-14 Proofs ~ 3 or 4 of each BU (42-56 BU)

POP QUEEN SET
* 12-14 Proofs ~ 5 to 9 of each BU (70-126 BU; up to 134 BU)

POP KING SET
* 12-14 Proofs ~ 10 to 19 of each BU (135 -266 BU; up to 269 BU)

POP POPE SET
* 12-14 Proofs ~ 20 or more of each BU (270 and up BU)

<u>**Contemplating Dollar Values:**</u> I would estimate that, as a non-binding assessment, at $22/oz fair dollar values should be at least double the Rank numbers of higher end POP SETs, growing larger as SET value increases.

Stack On Silver Lovers!

Notes:

Notes:

Notes:

____

____

____

____

____

____

____

____

____

Notes:

Notes:

*Only gold and silver have ever been real money;
everything else has been currency.
And today, silver is far more important
and undervalued than gold is.
Thus silver is the greatest investment opportunity
in the history of humanity.*